SCARBOROUGH C

D0476331

NORTH YORKSHIRE

❖

John A A Goodall PhD

Scarborough Castle stands on a massive promontory of rock that rises sheer-sided high above the North Sea. Today the medieval defences and keep form a spectacular crown to this natural stronghold, but they are relatively modern additions to a site that has been intermittently inhabited and fortified for nearly 3000 years. With its own anchorage, now the harbour, Scarborough has long been an important gateway to north-east England. During the Iron Age its first settlers traded widely and in the fourth century the Romans built a fortified signal station here, one of a coastal chain that watched for seaborne raiders.

The great medieval castle which developed on the headland figured prominently in national events throughout the Middle Ages and Tudor period. It was briefly abandoned in the early seventeenth century, but was reoccupied during the Civil War and twice besieged by Parliamentary forces. Subsequently the castle became one of a handful of permanently garrisoned fortifications in Britain. Its defences were most recently assaulted in 1914, when the castle and town were shelled by German warships.

QUICK TOUR OF THE CASTLE

4 MASTER GUNNER'S HOUSE PAGE 6
An early eighteenth-century house built for the master gunner of Scarborough's gun batteries

3 CASTLE GATE PAGE 6
The gateway to the plateau enclosure, now lost, closed the top end of the barbican

2 BARBICAN PAGE 4
The outer defence to the castle, built to fortify the causeway

5 HEADLAND PAGE 7
Protected on three sides by cliffs and on the other by the curtain wall, this natural stronghold is a huge 16 acres, the size of eight football pitches

6 SIGNAL STATION PAGE
The remains of a Roman watchtower, with a medieval chapel built over its foundation

ILLUSTRATION BY PETER DUNN

1 BARBICAN GATEHOUSE PAGE 4
This spans the narrow causeway of rock which is the only approach to the castle plateau

The numbers and page numbers refer to the tour starting on page 4

12 KEEP PAGE 14
Henry II's great tower, built 1159–69; the west wall collapsed after bombardment during the Civil War siege of 1645

13 VIEWING PLATFORM PAGE 20
Offers a fine view of the town and harbour, and of the curtain wall and massive double ditch below

11 INNER BAILEY PAGE 1
A small, fortified enclosure created in the twelfth century to surround the castle's earlies residential buildings

7 CURTAIN WALL PAGE 8
This defensive wall with towers was built by King John in 1202–12. Its southern end has been washed away by the sea

8 SALLY PORT PAGE 8
A small gate through which the garrison could pass to South Steel Battery further down the cliff

10 KING'S HALL PAGE 11
Beside King John's lodging, the great hall was the public chamber of his residence, where the royal household ate and slept

9 KING JOHN'S CHAMBER BLOCK PAGE 10
The ruins of a royal lodging, built by King John in 1210–11 and rebuilt as a barracks after 1745

❖ CONTENTS ❖

Published by English Heritage, 1 Waterhouse Square, 138-142 Holborn, London, EC1N 2ST. © English Heritage 2000. First published by English Heritage 2000. Photography by English Heritage Photographic Unit and copyright English Heritage unless otherwise stated.

Edited by Katy Carter. Designed by Pauline Hull. Picture research by Diana Phillips. Plans by Hardlines. Printed in England by Alderson Print Group. Reprinted 2003, 2004, 2006, 2007, 2008 Revised reprint 2010
C85 08/10 07555 ISBN 978 1 85074 786 4

Mixed Sources
Product group from well-managed forests and other controlled sources
www.fsc.org Cert no. TT-COC-002494
© 1996 Forest Stewardship Council
FSC

TOUR OF
THE CASTLE

❖

The following tour starts at the barbican and works clockwise around the plateau to finish in the inner bailey. The directions in *italic* type will help you find the main points of interest, but should you prefer to go your own way the bird's-eye view on page 2 and plan on page 36 will help orientate you. The numbers in the text below relate to key features on the bird's-eye view.

Having left the ticket office pause on the route up to the castle and look towards the keep above you.

THE BARBICAN (1 AND 2)

The diamond-shaped plateau of land on which Scarborough Castle stands is protected along three sides by cliffs and the sea. On the fourth side, facing towards the town, there is a massive double ditch overlooked by a medieval curtain wall with towers. The only approach to the plateau is along the narrow causeway on which you are now standing, a great bridge built over a natural spur of rock that crosses the double ditch dividing the town from the castle.

This approach, now no more than a winding road, was formidably defended in the Middle Ages. Surrounding the ticket office behind

Henry III's barbican bridge. The tower is all that remains of its gate. To either side of this there were originally drawbridges, now replaced with stone arches

one on either side of a central gate tower. This tower spanned the road and was closed with its own portcullis. Clustered around it, at the outer corners of the drawbridge pits, were four smaller turrets.

Extensive rebuilding makes it impossible to date the various medieval elements of the barbican with certainty. The first reference to a barbican occurs in 1175 and the foundations of a square tower which possibly belongs to this twelfth-century fortification lie beneath the ticket office. Most of the existing features, however, are later in date. The barbican gate tower was built by Henry III in 1243–5 and compares in design with such buildings as the Black Tower at Newcastle and the 1280s entrance to Conwy Castle.

you is a fortified enclosure with its own towers and gatehouse. From this point upwards the road was enclosed within walls 5.5m (18 ft) high, and these supported wall walks that allowed the garrison to overlook the ditch on either side. About halfway up the causeway the approach was interrupted by two drawbridges, set

Left: The barbican gatehouse, although much rebuilt, probably reflects the design of a thirteenth- or fourteenth-century original. An oddly shaped stone set in the left-hand tower is a much worn royal coat of arms which follows a form in use from about 1400

Above: The remains of Henry III's barbican gate tower. The zigzag division between rough and fine masonry marks the line of a staircase to the upper storey. This stood on the projecting stones around the rim

Left: The ruined barbican gate in 1789. At this time it still preserved an outer drawbridge, which had replaced the medieval original

SCARBOROUGH MUSEUMS

The present barbican defences had to be joined to the existing curtain wall enclosing the plateau. On the surviving (southern) side this was done by building the barbican wall up against an existing curtain tower. A doorway was then punched through the front of the tower to give access onto the new barbican wall walk

Continue up the hill until you are standing immediately beneath the keep.

THE CASTLE GATE (3)

Entrance from the barbican into the main castle enclosure on the headland plateau was through a gateway, now lost, set immediately beneath the keep. Extending to either side of this gateway was a fortified wall – or curtain – which, from at least the early thirteenth century, encircled the entire headland. Only the part overlooking the town still remains.

Walk past the keep and follow the path round to the left as far as the stone-built house.

MASTER GUNNER'S HOUSE (4)

This small house, attractively decorated with stepped gables, was purpose built in the early eighteenth century as the lodging for the master gunner serving the castle batteries. It belongs to a group of such houses built across the country in this period – for example in Walmer and Dover Castles in Kent – and testifies to Scarborough's continued military importance.

The building was much altered before 1821 and a plan of this date shows that it was arranged with a parlour and kitchen on the ground floor. Above were a pair of bed-

Above: A display niche in the Master Gunner's House, one of its surviving domestic fittings

Right: The Master Gunner's House

chambers and two attic rooms. Until the 1740s the cellar of the house may have served as a powder magazine. The building preserves a fine eighteenth-century wooden stair and display niche.

Follow the grass path across the headland (5) until you come to a cluster of ruins on the edge of the cliff.

THE ROMAN SIGNAL STATION AND CHAPEL OF OUR LADY (6)

When this area was excavated in the 1920s traces were found of three important phases of occupation. The earliest finds, of which nothing is now visible, were a series of Iron Age storage pits and post holes, dating to between 800 and 500BC. Built across these were the remains of a fourth-century Roman signal station and various medieval foundations, including those of a chapel. It is the combined remains of the Roman and medieval structures that form the confusion of walls, mounds and ditches visible today.

To distinguish the details of the Roman signal station, trace the outline of the grass-covered mounds and dips. These consist of three square-planned Roman features set one within the other, parts of which have been lost over the cliff. Working inwards there is a ditch, an enclosure wall, and the base of a tower. Excavation revealed

the bases for timber posts within the tower foundation, presumably supports for a floor, and also the bases of D-shaped towers at each corner of the enclosure wall. On the landward side of the station are the exposed foundations of its gateway, partly obscured by medieval walls.

There is much debate about the precise dating, appearance and function of this building, but its remains compare closely with similar fourth-century structures on the Yorkshire coast at Filey, Huntcliffe and Goldsborough. It was probably built in the 360s or 380s as one in a chain of lookout stations intended to warn of the approach of raiders.

The exposed stone foundations are largely medieval and remain incompletely understood. They belong to a chapel dedicated to Our Lady, which was rebuilt and extended at various times, and also to a domestic house, which has both medieval and later elements. The earliest chapel remains here have been dated to around the year AD1000 and are built over the foundations of the Roman tower. In the later Middle Ages the chapel is known to have been associated with a well, but confusingly two wells now exist on the site. The larger of these, set underground in a medieval vault, was probably the principal one. In the eighteenth century a water tank was built within this vault.

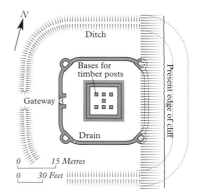

A plan of the Roman signal station, showing its three square-planned elements: The ditch, enclosure wall and central tower

BRITISH LIBRARY

Detail from the 1538 survey of the castle (see page 28), showing the well and chapel

Walk along the eastern edge of the plateau to the far corner, where the curtain wall overlooks the town.

Set above a massive double ditch and strengthened with towers, King John's curtain wall still dominates the town below. To the right, below the castle, is South Steel Battery, built in 1643 to command the harbour

THE CURTAIN WALL (7)

This surviving stretch of curtain wall, which extends along the whole length of the promontory overlooking the town, was built by King John between 1202 and 1212 and replaced an earlier line of twelfth-century defences.

In the 1730s a cliff collapse damaged the Cockhyll Tower – a large polygonal tower – at the southern extreme of the curtain, and this is now lost.

Sally port and South Steel Battery (8)

Just short of the present cliff edge, a small door or sally port passes through the curtain wall. Descending from it is a covered staircase set with musket loops, which leads to South Steel

Battery. This gun emplacement was built by the town in 1643 to command the harbour. It was enlarged in 1652–7, but it was probably not until 1745 that the sally port and fortified communication to the castle were built. The battery remained in use into the nineteenth century, but part of it had collapsed by 1847. Further erosion has rendered it unstable.

Begin to walk along the curtain wall towards the keep.

Wall towers

Apart from the Cockhyll Tower, the other medieval towers along the curtain wall still survive, although in a ruined and much altered state. Judging from their physical evidence, the process of constructing the curtain was interrupted at some stage. Where the inner bailey wall meets the curtain there is a change in the design of the towers. In the stretch running south from the inner bailey to the cliff, all the towers (bar two turrets added in the fourteenth century) are hollow internally, to allow for the insertion of floors. Originally these stood two storeys high, with arrow slits on each level, and were crowned with a battlemented wall walk. North of the same point, within the inner bailey, the curtain towers are solid and had no internal chambers, except perhaps at wall-walk level. This change in design suggests that the northern end of the curtain enclosing the inner bailey was built first. The break in construction possibly corresponds to the year 1206–7 when, for no apparent reason, the level of expenditure on the castle suddenly dropped to nothing.

Most of King John's towers along the curtain wall are D-shaped in plan. This form is very unusual in English castle architecture around 1200, when square or polygonal plans are more common, and illustrates how sophisticated the architecture of the castle was for its date.

Left: The sally port from the castle to South Steel Battery. The fortified stair to which this descends was probably built in 1745

An interior view of one of King John's curtain towers built between 1207 and 1212. The ruined back wall of the tower was added to the original structure, probably in the later thirteenth century, and is likely to have replaced an original timber back

An artist's reconstruction of King John's chamber block as it may have appeared in the thirteenth century. The king's inner chambers were on the upper floor and approached up two stairs, for which the foundations still survive.
(Reconstruction by Ivan Lapper)

To have a fire on the upper storey of a timber-floored building it was common to support its stone heath on a column of masonry built up from ground level. This is the base of one such column in the chamber block

KING JOHN'S CHAMBER BLOCK (9)

These ruins, popularly known as Mosdale Hall, belong to a royal lodging or chamber block built by King John and were under construction in 1210–11. In the manner typical of that period, the block was arranged as a two-storey building divided by a partition wall to create one large and one small room on each level. A curtain wall tower constructed on a polygonal plan at the north corner of the block provided an extra room opening off each floor. At the opposite (south) end of the block is a latrine pit.

All that survives today of this once impressive lodging is the basement, lit with windows along both sides. Its rooms possibly contained household offices. The lost upper floor was the principal storey, comprising the inner royal apartments, and may have included a chapel in the upper level of the tower. Both of its rooms were warmed by fires – the stone bases that supported the hearths of these are still visible – and, to judge from the projecting stone foundations at either end of the building, had separate external stairs and porches. The existing foundations are later additions to the building but probably reflect earlier arrangements.

This lodging was still in use as a royal chamber block in 1260, during Henry III's reign, and also in 1361, when a survey made for Edward III describes the 'Queen's Chamber' as being located here. A survey of 1538, however, indicates that the building was in ruins, as it remained for a further two centuries.

After the abortive Jacobite rebellion of 1745 – a rising in support of Charles Edward Stuart's claims to the English throne – the government decided to house a garrison within the castle. King John's chamber block was chosen as the site for a new barrack block. The medieval structure was cased in brick and adapted to create a building on three floors with separate sections, corresponding to the ancient internal partition wall, for officers and men (see page 33).

Badly damaged by German shelling in 1914, the barrack was demolished and the brickwork stripped away from all but the exterior of the curtain wall. Appropriately, this has preserved the prominence of this section of the castle from the exterior, a block of bright red brick in the gold of the medieval stone walls.

Go up the flight of steps at the end of the chamber block and turn right at the top. Within 10m (30 ft) are the lines of foundations in the grass.

THE KING'S HALL (10)

Until the mid-thirteenth century it was common for the principal elements of grand houses to stand distinct from one another. This was the case at Scarborough, and traced in the grass a short distance from King John's lodgings are the foundations of the great hall it served. This great hall was a public chamber, where the whole household ate and slept. It follows the classic medieval form for such buildings. The roof was supported internally on two rows of wooden posts. One of the square stone bases for these posts survives and the positions of the remainder are shown in the grass.

At the low or service end of the hall, in this case towards the north-west, were three doorways, which would originally have been concealed from the main body of the room by a screen. Those on each side served a buttery and pantry chamber, while that in the middle opened onto a corridor that ran to the kitchen. The kitchen is not aligned with the hall and is set apart to reduce the risk of fire. Also concealed behind the screen, but in the side wall of the hall, was the main entrance to the building. In the fourteenth century the hall, described as King's Hall in a survey of 1361, was divided in two by a wall which had an external buttress at either end.

BRITISH LIBRARY

In its original form, King John's chamber block was a prominent feature of the castle. This drawing from a survey of 1538 (see page 28) shows that its walls and tower rose high above the surrounding curtain and were decorated externally with buttresses and large windows

The remains of the King's Hall with its kitchen beyond. The line of the partition wall inserted in the fourteenth century is traced by the rubble foundation across the middle

The ditch surrounding the inner bailey. The foundations for one of the gates into the inner bailey can be seen projecting from the line of the wall. The stone base for its approach bridge also survives in the bottom of the moat

Walk towards the raised wall and ditch surrounding the keep.

INNER BAILEY DEFENCES

This wall and ditch, built by Henry II in the twelfth century, created an inner fortified enclosure within the plateau. There were two gates into this: one beside the Master Gunner's House to your right (north) and the other immediately to your left (south), of which traces can be seen in the ditch.

Turn right along the side of the moat and bank, and turn left at the path. With the keep to your right, go into the middle of the inner bailey.

THE INNER BAILEY (11)

Apart from the keep, there is little to see in the inner bailey, but a recent survey suggests that it developed in a remarkable way. It has been possible to trace the outlines of various lost buildings by measuring variations in the resistance of the ground to an electric current, a technique known as resistivity. Without excavation it is difficult to be sure of the results, but it appears that in the mid-twelfth century a regular courtyard of buildings existed on the site. One corner of this was demolished in the 1150s and the keep built onto it to create a domestic complex around a tower. A similar arrangement existed in the early twelfth century at Sherborne Castle (Dorset).

Fragments of carved masonry likely to be from the twelfth-century courtyard have been found re-used in King John's buildings in the castle, suggesting that John demolished the remainder after he began large-scale building operations at Scarborough in 1202. To replace them he constructed, as well as the lodgings and hall in the outer bailey, a second hall. This stood against the outer curtain wall at the southern corner of the inner bailey and adjoined one of its towers. Curiously, the foundations of the tower adjoining the hall are laid out to receive a D-shaped tower, but the building itself was actually polygonal in plan.

John's hall fell into ruin and was replaced by a kitchen, brewhouse and bakehouse in the fourteenth century. The remains of these, which include the base of an oven, can still be seen. There is also a well in the bailey, probably built in the twelfth century. It is over 46m (150 ft) deep and the stone lining descends 20.7m (68 ft) before giving way to natural rock.

The well in the inner bailey, with the keep beyond

ENGLISH HERITAGE/SKYSCAN BALLOON PHOTOGRAPHY

Set at a curious angle across the inner bailey, the great tower or keep was probably built onto the corner of a pre-existing courtyard of domestic buildings. These were later demolished by King John and the tower left isolated, as it is today

Right: The remains of the ruined forebuilding

Below: The keep looking east. In the base of the ruined west wall are the mouths of four latrine chutes. These indicate the existence of latrine chambers within the thickness of this wall on the upper floors

THE KEEP (12)

Even in its ruined state, the rugged outline of Henry II's great tower or keep, built between 1159 and 1169, still dominates the headland. It is a vast structure, over 27m (90 ft) high and with walls 3.5m (12 ft) thick. The present ruinous condition of the building is the result of an intense bombardment during the siege of 1645 (see page 31). This caused the collapse of the western wall and has left the building an open-sided masonry shell without floors, a roof or wall tops. Trying to piece together the original appearance of this building is a fascinating architectural puzzle. From it there emerges some impression of the former magnificence and ambition of the great tower.

Exterior

The keep originally took the form of a massive tower set on a broad sloping base. It was entered through a raised doorway on the first floor. As today, this doorway was approached up a flight of steps that rose along the south face of the keep. The original stair was less steeply pitched than the present one, and its upper section was formerly housed within a small tower, called a forebuilding, with three floors: a basement, entrance chamber and a chapel. This stood against the side of the keep and is now largely ruined.

As the centrepiece of Henry II's castle, the great tower was placed in the most commanding position on the headland. From here the tower not only overlooks the town but also the whole approach to the castle up the barbican, a menacing statement of royal authority. Its precise orientation was probably dictated by the lost courtyard buildings in the inner

❖ GREAT TOWERS ❖

SPECTRUM COLOUR LIBRARY

Scarborough's keep is one in a long tradition of similar castle buildings that developed in England after the Norman Conquest, once commonly known as 'great towers'. The grandest – which may still be seen at the Tower of London (the White Tower), Norwich, Rochester, Dover, Newcastle, and here at Scarborough – were square in plan and arranged with a forebuilding entrance.

Great towers were works of deliberate architectural virtuosity, intended to symbolise the power of their owners by their height, ornament and strength. So important were these towers that whole castles sometimes became identified by them. A case in point is London Castle, which is still popularly known by its medieval name as the Tower of London.

Such is the scale of many great towers that they remain celebrated landmarks to this day. Among the most important are the White Tower at the Tower of London (top), Rochester (middle) and Dover (bottom)

bailey, and entrance to it was deliberately complicated: in the twelfth century it would have been necessary to walk clockwise around the entire building before you could get into it, an impressive upwards spiral from the barbican to the forebuilding stair.

It is worth looking closely at the overall form of the tower. At each corner a turret rose above the battlemented walks along the top of the building. Viewed from a distance this created the effect of a cluster of miniature towers. Each corner of the building was decorated with a thin column. Apart from the side occupied by the forebuilding, every face of the great tower had a buttress-like projection down its centre. To the north and east these terminated at the level of the battlemented parapets as small, solid turrets. But on the lost, western side of the building, the feature encased a spiral stair and extended upwards to form a fifth projecting turret. A description of the tower in 1538 describes this stair turret as having a stone roof, probably a miniature spire (see p.19).

To either side of these central projections in the surviving walls there are pairs of windows. Today there are three levels of windows but a fourth, now blocked and only visible internally, also existed in the north face of the basement. The exterior decoration of the windows varies according to the use of the rooms they serve. In the storage area of the basement they are narrow slits; in the domestic chambers on the first and second floors the windows have twin openings divided by double columns and contained within semi-circular overarches; and on the stage above there are simpler pairs of round-headed openings.

Walk up the forebuilding stair and onto the platform within the keep.

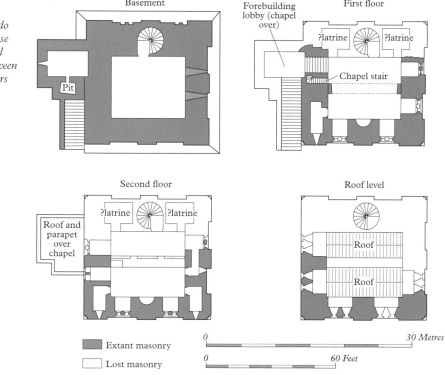

Floor plans of the keep. The forebuilding levels do not correspond with those of the keep, so the chapel within it is midway between the first and second floors

Basement

Pit

Forebuilding lobby (chapel over)

First floor

?latrine   ?latrine

Chapel stair

Second floor

Roof and parapet over chapel

?latrine   ?latrine

Roof level

Roof

Roof

Extant masonry

Lost masonry

0   30 Metres

0   60 Feet

Interior

If you turn your back on the gaping hole where the western wall of the keep once stood, it is still possible to appreciate how the interior of this great tower was arranged in the Middle Ages. From the platform on which you are standing, which is set fractionally below medieval first floor level, you can see how the windows, doors and fireplace (originally identical to the one above) appeared within each room. All the other internal levels and divisions, however, must be imagined. On the storey above, the position of the floor is clear from the various openings in the walls. You can also see that, just

beneath the centrally placed fireplace, the wall takes a step backwards so as to provide a seat for the lost floor timbers.

Dividing the first and second floors in half from west to east was a wall.

Its stumps are clearly visible between the windows to your left (north) and right (south). But this wall was not just a blank mass of masonry. The wall stumps at first floor level describe a curve, the lowest section of an arch which formerly spanned the whole floor. On second floor level to your right (south) there are similar remains of three smaller arches, all set at different levels. This arrangement shows that there would have been a doorway at the southern extreme of the wall, and a row of arches along the whole west face of the partition.

As well as the main rooms within the central space of the tower, there were also three chambers within the walls of the corner turrets, one on the first floor and two on the second. There may have been similar chambers in the lost corners of the building. There was an entrance to

The stump of the partition wall on the right (south side) of the second floor of the keep. Clearly visible are the stumps of three arches springing to the left, the remains of a lost doorway and blind arcade

The first floor fireplace (opposite) is damaged today. It was originally identical to the one on the floor above it

the chapel in the forebuilding from a stair rising beside the entrance door on the first floor. A broad spiral stair, connecting all the floors in the main part of the building, stood on the lost western side of the tower, where its lowest steps still survive. There were latrine chambers within the thickness of this wall on the upper floors (see illustration, page 14).

The uppermost level of Scarborough's keep is usually described as a fourth floor. However, many great towers had their roofs deeply countersunk within the stone structure, and often therefore had a dummy upper storey simply to conceal and enclose the roof. Although there is no clear evidence for the position of the roof at Scarborough, there are four principal reasons for suggesting that it followed this pattern. First, there are neither wall chambers nor a fireplace at this level. Second, there is no step seating for floor timbers. Third, keep roofs usually rested directly on the central partition wall of the building, and at Scarborough the surviving stumps of this wall prove that it did not extend above second floor level. Finally, the surviving north window to the western second floor chamber stands noticeably higher than the other openings on this level; had there been a third floor, this window would have encroached awkwardly into it. It must have stood, therefore, within the gable end of the original roof.

THE

A cutaway reconstruction of the keep in the twelft roof, typical of great towers in this period. (Recons

TWELFTH-CENTURY KEEP ❖

ury. Notice the countersunk
on by Ivan Lapper)

What would the great tower have been like to walk through in the twelfth century? Upon entering the keep a medieval visitor came into a large hall occupying the whole of the first floor and spanned by a wide arch. The half of this room beyond the arch was lit with four large windows and heated by a fire. In the half nearer the entrance there was probably only one large window, which still survives, at one end. Immediately beside the entrance, to the visitor's right, a stair in the thickness of the wall led to the chapel on the second floor of the forebuilding. In the centre of the lost west wall was a door to the principal stair, on either side of which were probably latrine chambers set in the thickness of the wall.

From the stair the medieval visitor could descend to the basement or climb to the upper storeys. On the next level up, the central space of the keep was divided in two by a wall that sat on the first floor arch below. The first of the two chambers, entered immediately from the stair, also probably had latrine chambers set in the west wall and large windows at either end. From this, the chamber beyond could be reached either via an arch at the far south end of the partition wall, or through a passage in the window recess at the opposite

(north) end of the room. The inner chamber was lit by two windows and warmed by a fire.

No documents reveal how the tower was used in the twelfth century, so we have to rely on these internal arrangements to work out how it functioned. They suggest that the building served as a grand residence. The first floor, large and relatively accessible, was probably a hall for the royal household, while the second formed a set of inner apartments for the king. Of the two chambers on the second floor, the one entered from the main stair was probably a public room, while that to the east was withdrawn and comfortably appointed. With two doorways between the two the king could either invite visitors through to see him (through the grand door in the partition wall) or appear ceremonially at one end of the outer chamber and greet them. There are similar arrangements in other great towers such as Dover.

The keep probably remained in use during royal visits until the end of the Middle Ages, but it is not clear how it related to the other residential buildings which developed in the castle. Most likely it remained the ceremonial focus of the castle and was used on formal occasions.

Walk down the forebuilding stairs and turn right towards the modern ramp to the viewing platform.

THE VIEWING PLATFORM (13)

There is a fine view from here of the town and harbour. Directly below is the church of St Mary, the parish church of Scarborough, which served as a Parliamentarian outpost during the Civil War in the siege of 1645. On your left (south), King John's thirteenth-century curtain wall, protected by the massive double ditch of the castle, extends down to the cliffs. The brick facing to the medieval walls shows at the point where the chamber block and eighteenth-century barracks stood. The ditch is a re-cutting of the natural slope and must have been insurmountable in its medieval form, when the ditch was both steeper and considerably deeper than at present. To your right (north) you can see how formidable were the defences of the barbican, with its bridge built in the 1240s.

When you leave the castle, if you turn left along Castle Dykes, the cliff path leading down to the harbour, you can fully appreciate the scale of King John's curtain wall and the double ditch.

The harbour and South Bay, seen from the viewing platform

HISTORY OF
THE CASTLE

❖

PREHISTORY

The earliest evidence of human activity on the promontory at Scarborough are fragments of Beaker pottery dating to between *c*.2100 and 1600BC. But it is only in the first millennium BC that there is clear evidence of a settlement here. Excavations on the headland have revealed pits, post holes and a wide variety of artefacts including axe heads, metalwork and pottery. These suggest two distinct periods of habitation, the first *c*.800BC and the second *c*.500BC. It is not clear how extensive either settlement was and sea erosion may have destroyed much evidence of them.

THE ROMAN SIGNAL STATION

In the late fourth century AD the Romans built a tower, fortified with a wall and ditch, on the headland. Finds of coins and pottery, and architectural similarity to other sites, suggest that this building was one in a set of signal stations erected along the north-eastern coast of Britain at this time. Remains of closely comparable structures, with towers, enclosure walls and ditches, survive at Filey, Huntcliffe and Goldsborough. Until recently scholars agreed that they were built by Count Theodosius in response to the so-called 'Barbarian Conspiracy' of 367. In that year an orchestrated invasion of the Western Roman Empire by barbarian tribes brought imperial authority in Britain to the verge of collapse, and the emperor, Valentinian, sent Theodosius to restore order. After a successful campaign to secure imperial government, Theodosius was active in strengthening Britain's defences and it was assumed that these forts were part of this work. More recently, however, they have been attributed to Magnus Maximus, a usurping emperor acclaimed by his troops and ruling Britain between 383 and 388.

A Bronze Age sword discovered on the headland in 1984. The Yorkshire Moors appear to have been widely settled during the Bronze Age, but the importance of Scarborough in this period is not yet clear

A reconstruction of the Roman signal station at Scarborough. The precise form of the building, which we only know of in plan, is open to very varied interpretation. Here the central tower is shown as a lighthouse with a beacon signal at the top. (Reconstruction by Ivan Lapper)

How the forts worked as signal stations is much debated. Some scholars think they were part of a chain, extending right down the coast from Hadrian's Wall, designed to watch for raiders and enable ships and military units to intercept their approach. But since only four have been identified for certain, there are big gaps in any such series and it has been necessary to infer the existence of several others, at places such as Whitby. One alternative suggestion is that the stations acted independently to warn inland settlements of attack.

VIKING SCARBOROUGH

The name Scarborough probably derives from Old Norse and means the stronghold of Skardi, or 'the man with the hare lip'. We cannot be sure who Skardi was, but he has been plausibly identified with a late tenth-century Viking raider, whose real name was Thorgils. Whoever its founder, Scarborough was evidently an important settlement in the Viking period and is mentioned in several Icelandic sagas. The earliest chapel on the castle promontory, which has been dated to around 1000, may have been associated with Viking Scarborough. Nevertheless, the settlement itself was probably focused around the harbour below. This is suggested by the first reliably documented historical episode involving the community there.

In 1066, while William the Conqueror waited with his army in Normandy for favourable winds to invade England, the exiled brother of King Harold, Earl Tostig, joined with the Norwegian king, Harald Hardrada, in an attempt to seize the English throne. The Norwegian fleet touched land north of Scarborough and then sailed down the coast towards it. One chronicler records that Hardrada, after meeting stiff resistance from the inhabitants, built a huge bonfire on the rock above the town and flung the burning brands onto the houses beneath. His men then slew many of the inhabitants. Hardrada was later killed and his army defeated at Stamford Bridge by King Harold on 25 September, three weeks before the Battle of Hastings.

THE EARLY CASTLE

SONIA HALLIDAY/LAURA LUSHINGTON

If it survived at all, Scarborough was slow to recover from Harald Hardrada's attack in 1066. It is not mentioned in the Domesday survey of 1086 and next comes to prominence after its re-establishment by Henry II in the mid-twelfth century as a borough prospering beneath the walls of a great royal castle. The founder of the castle was William le Gros, Count of Aumâle. He was created earl of York by King Stephen in 1138 and proceeded to establish himself as the unrivalled political master of the region. His work at Scarborough Castle, which probably began in the 1130s, was described later in the twelfth century by the chronicler, William of Newburgh. According to William, Aumâle was responsible for enclosing the plateau of the promontory with a wall and erecting a tower at the entrance, on the site of the present keep.

But within a few years of its foundation Aumâle lost his new stronghold. When Henry II acceded to the throne in 1154 he demanded the return of all royal castles and Scarborough, which was actually built on a royal manor, was one of these. At first Aumâle defied the new king, but when Henry marched to York he reluctantly submitted and Scarborough Castle passed into the hands of the Crown.

A ROYAL CASTLE

In 1159 Henry II began to rebuild the castle at Scarborough, an operation that coincided with the plantation of a new town beneath its walls. His work to the castle is documented in the so-called Pipe Rolls, the accounts of the royal exchequer. About £650 was spent on the castle over the next ten years, an enormous sum of money at that time - the King's income is estimated at £10,000 per annum. The principal object of expenditure was the keep, under construction from 1159 to 1169. William of Newburgh improbably claims that Henry built the new keep because Aumâle's tower, probably little more than 20 years old, was decayed with age. Much more likely, the new

Left: Henry II, depicted in thirteenth-century stained glass at Canterbury Cathedral

Royal building operations as depicted by the thirteenth-century monk chronicler of St Albans, Matthew Paris

TRINITY COLLEGE LIBRARY, DUBLIN (MS 177, FOL 59V)

❖ MONARCHS ON THE MOVE ❖

Medieval kings were perpetually moving around, billeting themselves and their retinues either in royal manors and castles, or in those of their subjects. They took with them all their personal belongings, which were unpacked to furnish any building in which they stayed. In the early twelfth century the king and his mobile household constituted the central organ of administration and rule. Gradually, however, departments of government – such as the Exchequer – were permanently established near London, in Westminster. Although individual offices might separate themselves from the household, the monarch remained the centre of power and access to him was a vital element in securing political influence.

The extent, scale and purpose of royal progresses varied immensely between reigns, but in times of peace, it was typical for kings to visit a core of favourite residences with a relatively small household. Virtually without exception these core residences lay in the south-east of England and were associated with hunting parks. However, at times of political difficulty or war progresses could go to every corner of the realm and involve very large numbers of people. John is known to have visited Scarborough several times and seems to have developed it, along with Knaresborough, as a major royal castle to control Yorkshire.

Left: A king dining with his household, from an early fourteenth-century manuscript

BRITISH LIBRARY MS ROYAL 14.E.III, FOL. 89

---

keep was intended to advertise the fact that the castle had changed hands. Henry II also enclosed the keep and its surrounding courtyard of domestic buildings with the inner bailey wall.

These changes proved to be a foretaste of yet more extensive alterations by King John between 1202 and 1212. The Pipe Rolls show that he spent £2291 on Scarborough during his reign, more than on any other individual castle in the kingdom. John's operations seem to have fallen into two distinct stages: first, the creation of an outer wall to the inner bailey in 1202–6, and second, the extension of that wall down to the cliff in 1207–12. During the second stage he also constructed a hall in the inner bailey and the new royal

BRITISH LIBRARY COTTON MS VIT.A.XIII. FOL.5V

chamber block with its separate great hall in the outer bailey.

Despite its importance to King John, the castle played little part in the civil war at the close of his reign. It was held by his loyal supporter, Geoffrey de Neville, and in 1215 its well-supplied garrison comprised ten knights, 72 sergeants and 13 crossbowmen.

John's son, Henry III, was active in provisioning and maintaining the castle through-out his reign. Exposed as it was to the action of the sea and extreme weather, repair was an almost continuous and vastly expensive operation. A tempest of 1237, for example, carried away the roofs of several castle buildings and in both 1241 and 1242 there were collapses of wall. The following year, in 1243, Henry also strengthened the barbican,

the fortified entrance of the castle, rebuilding it with the present great bridge and a double drawbridge tower.

At the end of Henry III's reign Scarborough Castle was one of the greatest fortresses in England. Its importance is reflected by its nomination, along with the castles of Dover, Nottingham, Bamburgh and Corfe, as a bargaining counter in the peace arrangements of 1265 between Henry III and his rebellious barons. After Henry's death in 1272, Edward I continued to use the castle as a royal lodging. In 1275 he held court and council at Scarborough and visited again in 1280. Prisoners from Edward's Scottish wars were also held here. In 1312 it was briefly the scene of a siege when Edward II's favourite, Piers Gaveston, took refuge here (see page 26).

Left: King John developed the existing defences at the castle and spent more money on Scarborough than on any other castle in his realm

This view of the barbican gatehouse (left) and bridge (right) shows the vast scale of the outer defences to the castle, strengthened by Henry III

PIERS GAVESTON

When still Prince of Wales, the future Edward II became closely attached to Piers Gaveston, a young man from Gascony in France. Gaveston was disliked by many of the nobility and was sent into exile in 1307 after a dramatic quarrel between Edward and his father, Edward I. The prince had demanded that his favourite be shown particular marks of favour and the king, furious at the request, drove him from the room, tearing out handfuls of his son's hair. When his father died, one of Edward's first acts was to recall Gaveston, who quickly became the object of bitter controversy between the new king and his barons. Edward's incompetence in government, combined with his infatuation, provoked the barons to demand that Gaveston be banished. In 1308 Gaveston was sent into exile, but he returned the following year.

In 1312, after further confrontations, Edward went to the north of England with Gaveston to escape his opponents. His enemies acted quickly. Most of the royal household was captured in a surprise attack on Newcastle, from which Edward and Gaveston only just escaped. Gaveston then went on to Scarborough Castle, where he was besieged. A shortage of supplies forced him to surrender within a fortnight. He gave himself up with promises of safe conduct, but while he was being escorted back to the south an inveterate enemy, the Earl of Warwick, seized and summarily beheaded him, to the delight of an assembled crowd.

An early fourteenth-century depiction of a castle under siege. Medieval sieges were often conducted with a brutality and ferocity ill-conveyed by such images

BRIDGEMAN ART LIBRARY (BL ADD. MS 10294, FOL. 81B)

THE LATE MEDIEVAL CASTLE

During the fourteenth and fifteenth centuries the castle underwent little change. In 1308 Lord Percy and his wife were granted licence to reside in the castle and the family continued to live here intermittently for at least the next 40 years, undertaking minor repairs and building a bakehouse, brew-house and kitchen in the inner bailey.

To judge from the evidence of occasional surveys of the fabric, the buildings were generally dilapidated and only repaired in extreme need. In this, Scarborough was typical of many royal castles. Visits by the king were now few and far between and without this incentive to maintain the buildings, the cost of repairs grew to a point that a hard pressed treasury was only likely to pay for what was essential.

Unscrupulous constables and keepers probably added to the damage caused by age and the weather, removing valuable building materials and dressing up the loss as damage. The section of wall, for example, recorded by a clerk in 1361 as having collapsed and conveniently disappeared into a cloud of sand, sounds suspiciously as if it was quarried away.

The last king to stay in the castle was Richard III. In 1484 he resided here while assembling a fleet to resist the expected invasion of Henry Tudor, later Henry VII.

THE CASTLE UNDER THE TUDORS

Even in its dilapidated state, Scarborough Castle continued to play an important role in times of crisis during the sixteenth century. In October 1536 there began one of the largest popular uprisings in English history, the so-called Pilgrimage of Grace. The northern counties of England, disaffected by economic problems and united in opposition to Henry VIII's religious changes – in particular the enforced suppression of the monasteries – rose up in revolt. Like all medieval rebels, the leaders of the Pilgrimage pledged loyalty to the Crown but demanded a redress of grievances. Henry's response was devious but effective. Unable to meet the rebellion with force he made promises, waited for the Pilgrims to disperse and then vengefully struck back early in 1537. Many of those involved were publicly executed.

Scarborough played an important role in these events. Upon the outbreak of the uprising, the constable of the castle, Sir Ralph Eure, declared his support for the king and was almost immediately besieged by an army of locals. A truce struck on behalf of the king at York on 28 October brought hostilities in Scarborough to a brief halt, but shortly afterwards a ship loaded with supplies for the castle was seized by the rebels and the blockade resumed.

A captain of the Pilgrimage of Grace, John Wyvill, was hanged in chains at Scarborough in 1537. This detail from the 1538 survey of the town (see over) may show his body hanging from the gallows

BRITISH LIBRARY

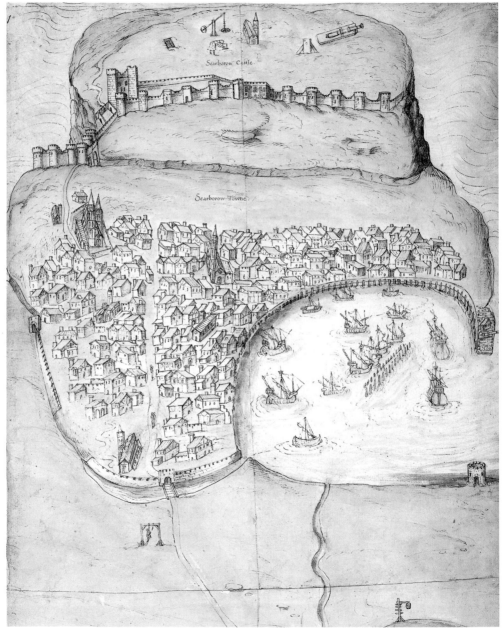

Scarborow Castle.

Scarborow Towne.

BRITISH LIBRARY MS COTTON AUG I. ii. FOL I

The attack was clearly determined and a survey of the castle made in 1538 records damage done to it by gunfire. Nevertheless, the castle was held successfully against assault. Ralph's reward from the king included the guardianship of the castle for life.

Twenty years later the castle was again involved in a doomed plot against the Tudor monarchy. On 25 April 1557 Thomas Stafford, believing that he could incite a popular revolt against Queen Mary, seized the castle and proclaimed himself Protector of the Realm. Some authorities claimed that he took the castle by stealth, others that he and his men simply wandered in and took control of the gates. The earls of Shrewsbury and Westmorland took the castle within six days, and Stafford was easily captured. Taken to London, he was tried and convicted for high treason, and was hanged and quartered at Tyburn on 28 May. His accomplices were executed at Scarborough and their bodies boiled and tanned for public exhibition. One result of the plot was that the governor of Scarborough was required to live in the castle to help guarantee its security. During the Northern Rising of 1569 – the attempt by some Catholic earls to unite the north in support of Mary Queen of Scots,

who was being held prisoner in England – Elizabeth I established a garrison at Scarborough. This was maintained until at least 1602.

The accession of James I in 1603 and the gradual political unification of England and Scotland prompted a revision of royal policy with regard to castles in the north of England. Without fear of Scottish invasion several important castles were parcelled out into private hands. Scarborough was purchased by a prominent local family, the Thompsons, and its land was rented as pasture; its days as a fortress seemed at an end.

THE CIVIL WAR

In September 1642, during the opening hostilities of the Civil War between Charles I and his Parliament, a local gentleman, Sir Hugh Cholmley, was sent with a commission to raise a regiment and hold Scarborough for Parliament. According to Cholmley's own vivid narrative of events, this force successfully occupied both the town and castle and was active in local skirmishes with Royalist forces for the next five months. But in that time Cholmley became disillusioned by Parliament and he was persuaded to change sides. Scarborough was an invaluable possession for the Royalist cause.

Opposite: This bird's-eye view of Scarborough was drawn in 1538 for Henry VIII as part of a military survey of the coast. Among the curiosities it shows are the two friary churches, demolished shortly afterwards. Notice the beacon at the bottom right of the picture and the cannon on the castle headland

Sir Hugh Cholmley, governor of Scarborough, from a portrait dated 1633. He was the central figure in the fortunes of Scarborough during the Civil War and his memoirs, written in exile in Rouen, France, tell the story of Scarborough during the events of 1642–5

NORTH YORKS LIBRARY (SCARBOROUGH)

This reconstruction by Ivan Lapper shows the collapse of the west wall of the keep during the siege of 1645. An eye-witness wrote: 'The fall of the tower was a very terrible spectacle, and more sudden than expected ... there were near twenty persons on top of the tower when it cleft, yet all got into the standing part except two.'

Charles I was dependent upon money, munitions and soldiers from the Continent, and his principal army in the north, at York, had no harbour to allow the passage of supplies. Scarborough was also of great strategic importance in controlling coastal trade.

When Cholmley declared his backing for the king his garrison consisted of 600 foot soldiers, 100 horsemen and 100 dragoons, or mounted soldiers. Those who chose to were allowed to leave, but not more than 20 did so. Immediately following this change of allegiance the castle was bloodlessly recaptured and then lost by Parliament. This happened while Cholmley was at York on a visit to Charles I. While he was away 40 seamen, acting for Parliament and under the command of Cholmley's cousin Captain Browne Bushell, surprised the guard at night and took the castle. On hearing the news, Cholmley rushed back to Scarborough and successfully

NORTH YORKS LIBRARY (SCARBOROUGH)

persuaded his relation to return the castle to him. For the next two years, between March 1643 and 1645, Scarborough served as an important Royalist base and its interception of shipping began to inflict serious coal shortages on London.

In 1644, however, the battle of Marston Moor shattered the king's cause in the north and Parliamentary forces began to close in on the remaining Royalist strongholds in the area. Cholmley began to prepare for a siege at Scarborough, but his situation was not easy. He did not have the forces to defend the town and lacked adequate provisions. When the Parliamentarian general, Lord Fairfax, approached the town in August 1644, Cholmley entered into negotiations for surrender in order to buy himself time for preparation. His proposed terms – which included the demand that he appoint his own successor as governor to the castle – were outrageous, yet they were seriously considered by Parliament.

The extra time won by this ruse proved to be of critical value when the siege, commanded by Fairfax's Lieutenant-General Sir John Meldrum, began. Sir Hugh was able to hold the town for three weeks before retreating into the castle on 18 February. Meldrum then tried to bully and cajole Cholmley into surrender but was eventually forced to bring up a siege train of guns, including one massive piece capable of firing a 64 pound ball. The church of St Mary below the castle was occupied by the besiegers as one outpost, but to judge from the damage inflicted on the keep the principal battery must have been on the rocky outcrop to the west of the castle. While setting up his guns there Meldrum toppled over the cliff trying to save his hat from the wind. Astonishingly, he survived the fall, but he was not on his feet again for six weeks.

When Meldrum recovered, the bombardment began. It was so intense that within three days the massive walls of the keep sheared and half the building collapsed. An assault followed, but it was repulsed, the first of several close and bloody engagements in the early part of the siege. Meldrum was killed shortly afterwards, shot through the stomach, in one of these attacks. The siege then changed character as the Parliamentary forces began to blockade the castle, which was now bombarded both by sea and land. In time, Cholmley ran out of gunpowder, then money and finally food. Reduced by casualties and scurvy, at the end of five months there were only 25 soldiers fit for duty. Cholmley surrendered on 25 July 1645.

'When he [Cholmley] wanted money and could not borrow ... he made use of plate [silverware] which was cut into pieces ... some of them had the stamp of a broken castle with this inscription "Caroli fortuna resurgam" [The fortune of Charles shall resurge].' Some of the improvised siege currency described in Cholmley's memoirs still survives, stamped with its value which was calculated by weight

But this was not the end of Scarborough's service in the Civil War. Parliament ordered the repair of the castle and established a permanent garrison of 100 men, as well as 60 gunners for the batteries commanding the harbour. This force was put under the command of a trusted Parliamentarian, Colonel Boynton. But Parliament failed to pay the garrison and on 27 July 1648, when the Civil War flared up again, Boynton declared his loyalty to the imprisoned king by flying a red standard from the battlements. This time Parliament pressed home the siege of the castle with all possible speed and in December Boynton was forced to surrender. Instructions were now given that the castle be

An early eighteenth-century engraving of Scarborough by Samuel Buck

damaged so as to put it beyond use – a process known as slighting – but opposition from the town preserved it from destruction.

PRISON AND BARRACK

Immediately after the Civil War, during continued hostilities with the Dutch, the castle, harbour batteries and garrison were kept in a state of defence. Nevertheless, in 1653 the Dutch Admiral De Witt sailed a small fleet into Scarborough bay and fired at a convoy of coal ships which were cowering against the shore under the protection of the batteries and nine men-of-war.

From the 1650s the castle served as a prison. Among those held here

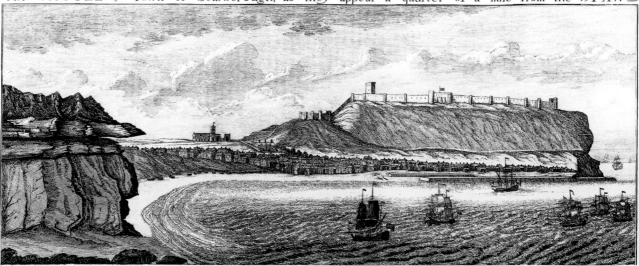

The CASTLE & Town of Scarborough, as they appear a quarter of a mile from the SPAW

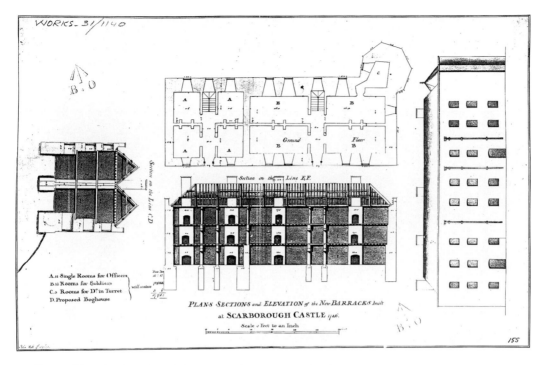

WORKS- 31/1140

A.11 Single Rooms for Officers
B.12 Rooms for Soldiers
C.2 Rooms for D° in Turret
D. Proposed Boghouse

PLANS SECTIONS and ELEVATION of the New BARRACKS built
at SCARBOROUGH CASTLE 1746.

Scale 8 Feet to an Inch

155

The plans, sections and elevation of the new barracks as built in 1746 within the remains of King John's chamber block. The officers' rooms were to the left and those of the other ranks to the right

was George Fox, the founder of the Society of Friends, known as the Quakers. He was held in the Cockhyll Tower between April 1665 and September 1666, the longest of his many spells of imprisonment, and complained of the appalling conditions: *'I had neither chimney nor firehearth. This being to the seaside and much open, the wind drove the rain in forcibly, so that the water came up over my bed and ran about the room that I was fain to skim it up with a platter'*.

By 1688 the castle garrison had been run down and during the 'Glorious Revolution' – the sequence of events which led to James II's replacement on the throne by William of Orange and Mary – Scarborough was seized by the Earl of Danby on behalf of the Protestant prince of Orange. In the event, the castle played no part in the subsequent overthrow of James II, and nothing was immediately done to improve or repair its defences.

Subsequent military surveys of the coast continue to mention the castle, but it was not until the Jacobite Rebellion of 1745 – the final, failed attempt to restore a Stuart to the throne – that any significant measures were taken to restore Scarborough. As a result of the rebellion a barracks block was constructed within the walls of King John's chamber block, and this remained in use into the mid-nineteenth century. Despite such precautions Scarborough remained vulnerable to attack and in 1779, the American commander and privateer John Paul Jones engaged and defeated two men-of-war in the bay beneath the castle.

❖ THE SPA TOWN ❖

From the 1660s Scarborough became famous as a fashionable spa town, or 'Spaw' as it was called. The water from a spring in the cliffs was said to have medicinal qualities which, according to its most enthusiastic advocates, offered relief from almost every complaint. Great numbers of people flocked to the resort, which flourished throughout the eighteenth century. Sea bathing, then an unknown practice, was also added to the pleasures of the place at this time. The influx of outsiders transformed the town, and several elegant terraces of house sprang up to accommodate visitors.

Detail from a 1735 engraving of Scarborough by John Setterington. It is the earliest known record of the use of bathing machines

This photograph of c.1890 shows visitors to Scarborough Castle using the moat for a little target practice

THE GERMAN SHELLING

On the morning of 16 December 1914, in the opening months of the First World War, the sea fog around Scarborough lifted to reveal three German warships off the coast. One was laying mines in the distance, but two battle cruisers, the *Derrflinger* and *Von der Tann*, were in the bay itself and at 8.05am they opened fire on the town and castle. The firing continued for 15 minutes and then, after a lull, the ships moved off at speed, firing again as they went. During this short attack, in which more than 500 shells were fired, 17 civilians were killed and more than 80 seriously wounded. British public opinion was shocked and outraged by the bombardment: 'Remember Scarborough!' became a rallying cry for recruiting officers across the nation.

NORTH YORKS LIBRARY (SCARBOROUGH)

GERMAN RAID DEC 16TH 1914 SHELLS EXPLODING ON THE CASTLE WALLS SCARBOROUGH.

This retouched photograph shows German shells exploding on the castle walls in 1914. The barracks block was severely damaged during this attack

THE CASTLE TO THE PRESENT DAY

In 1920 Scarborough Castle was taken into state guardianship by the Ministry of Works. Under its ownership the eighteenth-century barracks block, which had been badly damaged in the German bombardment, was demolished and the medieval fabric which it incorporated was exposed to view. Since 1984 the site has been in the care of English Heritage.

Further Reading

Binns, J. 'Scarborough and the Civil Wars, 1642–51', *Northern History*, **22**, 1986.

Binns, J. 'Scarborough and the Pilgrimage of Grace', *Transactions of the Scarborough Archaeological and Historical Society*, **33**, 1997.

Binns, J. (ed.) '*The Memoirs and Memorials of Sir Hugh Cholmley of Whitby, 1600–57'*, *Yorkshire Archaeological Society Record Series*, 153, 2000.

Douet, E. *British Barracks, 1600–1914*, HMSO, 1998.

Edwards, M. (ed.) *Scarborough 966–1966*, Scarborough and District Archaeological Society Research Report 6, 1966.

Firth, C. (ed.) 'Sir Hugh Cholmley's narrative of the siege of Scarborough, 1644-45', *English Historical Review*, 32, 1917, pp. 568-87

Grenville, J., Clark, J. and Giles, K. *Scarborough Castle Conservation Report*, 1999, unpublished.

Rowntree, A. (ed.) *The History of Scarborough*, London, 1931.

Wilson, P. R. 'Aspects of the Yorkshire signal stations', in V. A. Maxfield and M. J. Dobson (eds.), *Roman Frontier Studies*, 1989.

Acknowledgements

Thanks to Jonathan Clark, who has generously passed on much information from his doctoral thesis, and Jeremy Ashbee.

PLAN OF SCARBOROUGH CASTLE

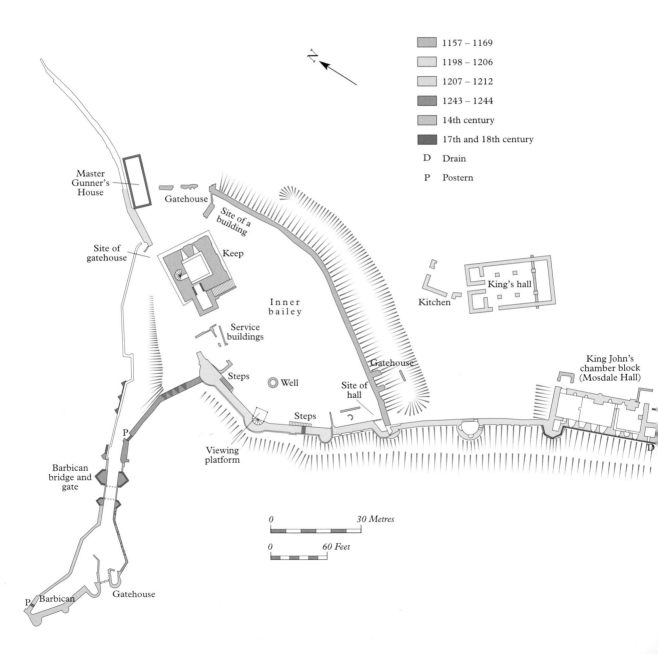

1157 – 1169
1198 – 1206
1207 – 1212
1243 – 1244
14th century
17th and 18th century

D   Drain
P   Postern

Master Gunner's House

Gatehouse

Site of a building

Site of gatehouse

Keep

Inner bailey

Service buildings

King's hall

Kitchen

Steps

Well

Gatehouse

King John's chamber block (Mosdale Hall)

Site of hall

Steps

Viewing platform

P

Barbican bridge and gate

D

0   30 Metres

0   60 Feet

P   Barbican   Gatehouse